MW00414859

ISBN 9781074063894

Citations from the Bible are from English Standard
Version (ESV), New International Version (NIV), and
New King James Version (NKJV) translations

Editor - Mim Harrison
Cover and book design - Hannah Hinson
Cover photo - Tom Milne, Milne Photography
Author's photo - Michael McCall

To my people. Thank you…

Mom and Dad

Cristal Tiscareno

Rachael McCall

Eugene and Victoria Park

Steve and Deby Hergenrader

Isaiah Green

Matthew and Alyssa Garvin

Amber Ramirez

Andrew and Jennifer Young

William Cherry

"MOM WHAT HAPPENED TO HER?"

"Mom, What Happened to Her?"

ENVISIONING A MORE INCLUSIVE CHURCH

TERRA LYNCH

Contents

STEREOTYPED

I can feel the stares of people. Would you believe me if I said they do not bother me? Even when I was young, I did not mind people's watchful curiosity. As early as age six, I recall being conscious of people's negative reactions. Instead of letting it make me feel insecure, I would smile to put them at ease.

I understand why they stare—I am different from the average person's idea of normal. I have a condition called cerebral palsy, which means my muscles are constantly tight. Even when I'm not moving, there's still some degree of tightness throughout my body. So, I imagine that I look like I'm in a constant state of struggle. Because of this, my posture and gait are different from that of the average person. So at this point in my life, I expect the gawking, as well as the questions that may follow. Typically, adults will look at me surreptitiously, if they look at me at all. Children often bluntly state whatever is on their mind. When they are curious, nothing will stop kids from finding out what they want to know. Interestingly enough, they almost always formulate the common question about me in the same way.

"Mom, what happened to her?"

More often than not, the parent replies in a panicked and uncomfortable whisper, "Shhh, honey—don't look, don't stare," trying to censor her child's curiosity before possibly offending me.

What kids really want to know is why I walk around with crutches, or why I use a wheelchair. Children usually associate these mobility devices with someone who is injured, so the logical question is to wonder what "happened" to me. But when the adults either overreact or try to avoid answering, children get the sense that their seemingly neutral inquiry is taboo. This, I believe, is how stigmas regarding disability develop and are perpetuated.

Social observations suggest that humans tend to draw conclusions about people's personality and character based on their looks, or their likes. I myself am guilty of this. Whether it's the type of music they listen to, the food they eat, or the team they root for,

I have often allowed these things to influence my impression of others.

When things are different or out of the norm, these perceived abnormalities often produce fear, and fear can encourage avoidance. When it comes to the topic of disability, I've witnessed three main types of reactions:

- Fear – feeling insecure or uncertain about how to interact with someone with a disability. This person might want to interact, yet has minimal knowledge of how to do it. One time, I was walking into my physical therapist's office and a lady who looked to be in her mid-70s gasped. I turned to look behind me to see what she was gasping at, thinking she had seen a nasty spider, but there was nothing behind me. She made that noise because of me!

- Distance/Avoidance – completely avoiding potential interactions. This person changes his or her behavior to avoid connecting or communicating with someone with a disability. Once, when I was trying to purchase a ticket to see a movie, I asked a young gal if she and her group of friends were in line at the box office. She didn't say anything, looked right at me, and then looked away quickly. But she never gave a response.

- Pity – feeling sorry for someone with a disability, assuming the person is constantly suffering or struggling, and therefore desiring to give relief or aid, or to show compassion. When I was eating out at a burger joint with my mom, I passed a girl and her mom. I heard her say, "Mom, I feel bad for her."

When the world looks at me, they expect to see someone who is defeated. I should be angry, sad, and incapable. These emotions and reactions are the typical responses to suffering. But when people actually get to know me, they find someone who is quite the opposite. In no way do I feel like I was dealt a bad card in life because I lack the ability to walk on my own. The story I have to tell is not filled with great sorrow or despair. In fact, I have been blessed beyond measure. I have a loving family and supportive friends from all around the world. None of them see my disability – they see me. Not all people who experience a disability are given the opportunity to see how they can be of value, not only to society but also to the Kingdom of God. I am one of the lucky ones who has the opportunity to live out that calling, as I've been able to serve alongside my able-bodied brothers and sisters in Christ in several different capacities. From mission trips, to volunteering in Sunday school, to serving on the social media team at my church in Fresno, California, there's always been somewhere for me to serve. I've never felt like I could not contribute to bringing people to know Christ because of my cerebral palsy.

Jesus's instruction for the Christian life is not implicitly directed toward one specific group of people. He calls on us all to be "Fishers of Men" (Matthew 4:19), and therefore to not exclude those whom society considers to have some sort of handicap from this calling.

But what if the Church is not giving the disabled population the opportunity to be obedient to God's purpose and calling?

I am writing this book to redefine the word disability. I want the Church to understand that disability is anything that separates a person from others. Everyone is affected by disability, whether they realize it or not. Yet God has intended all of his followers to serve Him in the church. So those with an actual diagnosis shouldn't be expected to simply show up as a spectator.

For you formed my inward parts; you knitted me together in my mother's womb. I praise you, for I am fearfully and wonderfully made. Wonderful are your works; my soul knows it very well. My frame was not hidden from you, when I was being made in secret, intricately woven in the depths of the earth. Your eyes saw my unformed substance; in your book were written, every one of them, the days that were formed for me, when as yet there was none of them.

Psalm 139:13-16

CHAPTER 1

NOT A MISTAKE

"You're not mad at God?"

It was my junior year at Clovis West High School in Fresno, California. I was leaving school for the day when I heard a voice shout loudly to me from behind. I was taken aback. I wondered if I had heard him right, and if I should bother even answering. But my curiosity got the better of me, and I quickly turned around to meet the voice.

A young man wearing a black hoodie and black, low-hanging jeans was looking directly at me.

He jabbed a finger in the direction of my body and questioned me again. "You're not mad at God?"

In disbelief, I replied, "No. Why would I be?"

"Because you're in a wheelchair," he said.

So that's what this was about. I smiled and replied, "No. God doesn't make mistakes."

"Oh, okay. Thanks." And with that, he nodded and walked back to the group of people he was with. He seemed unimpressed with my answer. His response was almost comical, considering he was so abrupt and demanding in the way he tried to get my answer. My response may have seemed naïve, a cliché, or just flat-out stupid to him.

I had occasionally seen my interrogator walking around campus. We didn't have the same friends or hang out in the same places, so I never suspected he cared about the things of God or had the slightest interest in my life. People ask me strange questions all the time, and by default, my brain filed his remark into the category of "weird disability questions people ask." But because his question was related to God rather than the usual questions people asked regarding my disability, the interaction I had with him at school that day still affects me to this day. He gave me a very clear picture of how people perceive disability.

It wasn't until I started writing this book that I realized that a general perception about disability is that it is equivalent to suffering. In some cases, that can be true. Because my life is blatantly marked by physical limitations, people think I should be mad at God for my situation. To an unbeliever, it is often hard to believe in a God who would allow suffering and affliction to plague those He claims to love. His word, however, makes it abundantly clear that sufferings and trials in this world are the result of the brokenness that was introduced to the world in the Garden of Eden. And the merciful God we serve took this brokenness and redeemed this suffering into something that draws us closer to Him, and lifts our eyes to see what will truly and completely satisfy.

Ironically, what the young man on my high school campus didn't realize is the "suffering" he observed in my outward appearance is not at all what causes me to suffer. We all have afflictions that cause hardships in our lives—some are physical, some are emotional, and some are spiritual. But none of these afflictions are mistakes on God's part, nor are they the result of His lack of care or involvement. I know God created me intentionally; He designed every detail of who I am for a specific reason.

In 1987 my parents welcomed a two-pound, five-ounce baby girl into the world. When I asked my mom what it was like when I was born, I expected to hear a traumatic story, considering I was supposed to born in November but came in August. Mom said she felt a lot of pain, and knew something was wrong. But despite the high stress situation my parents found themselves in, Mom explained that she and Dad were surprisingly calm. Or maybe they were in such shock, they had no choice, but to just go with it. "We just knew you were coming," Mom said. She expressed that she felt both scared and excited upon my arrival. Being the first and only child of my parents, they had to deal with nerves as most first-time parents do, but the circumstances surrounding my birth were more serious than I think they were ever prepared for.

My heart and lungs were not yet fully developed, and I needed a machine to help me breathe. In addition, doctors noticed that I had a cardiac murmur, which led to finding that I had patent ductus arteriosus (PDA). It meant that doctors had to go in and close the hole in my aorta, the artery that carries blood from the heart to the rest of the body. Following this procedure, I was in the NICU, or neonatal intensive care unit, for sixteen days. I wasn't allowed to go home until I weighed four pounds.

Even after having complications at birth, I initially did not go home with a diagnosis. Because the PDA procedure went smoothly, all looked good. As time went on, though, my parents noticed I was not meeting the typical milestones of infant development. Mom and Dad would clear out the living room floor for me to practice sitting up on my own. Dad would set me down, but I would instantly flop over to my side. I didn't have the strength or ability to sit up on my own. I wouldn't crawl, I would just lie on my stomach. Concerned, my parents took me to the doctor, where

I was given the official diagnosis of cerebral palsy (CP), a brain disorder that causes my movements to be impaired. Although all babies are at risk for CP, as a premature baby, I was even more at risk since my body had not finished developing. To this day, I do not know whether my CP was caused by part of my brain failing to develop properly or because I suffered an injury to my brain before, during, or after my birth.

As a child, I knew there was something different about me. In kindergarten, I remember sitting on the floor with my classmates, getting ready to listen to the teacher read a story aloud to us. I was sitting "criss-cross applesauce" just like everyone else, except for the fact that I was surrounded by the big metal frame of my walker. I remember peering through the bars of my walker and thinking, "Oh, they don't have one [a walker] like me." But I did not think twice about it after that. It was merely an observation; not something that made me feel I was better or worse than my classmates.

I also saw a physical therapist once a week in hopes of improving my strength, flexibility, and range of motion. I feel having to do PT every week made my differences seem more amplified than the equipment that helped me walk. I knew other kids didn't have to work on getting stronger, stretching out their legs, or practice standing. They were already able to do what I had to work on every week. But these differences never seemed to prevent me from doing what I wanted to do. I loved to play with my friends. I was also involved in gymnastics, dance, wheelchair basketball, tennis, and horseback riding.

Because cerebral palsy did not hold me back in my childhood, I wasn't interested in learning anything about my condition. My parents never explained my condition to me because I never asked. If there was something I couldn't do because my disability made it difficult, I would ask my parents for help, or we would figure out a way to get it done. They never treated me like I was incapable or a special case. I remember walking through the mall one day with Mom, focused on window-shopping and not watching where I was going. I walked straight into a metal pole and fell straight backward. As the loud clang of the metal rang out, I looked up at my mom. Instead of gushing sympathy or concern, she asked, "Why did you do that?" This might sound harsh, but it is reflective of how my mom treated me like any other child. She didn't view me as someone who was fragile or broken, which helped me to view myself that same way. So I'm a little different. Who cares? I can still do everything my friends can!

It wasn't until I was older that I felt embarrassed not knowing how to answer people who wanted to know the details of my disability. They would ask me to explain what cerebral palsy was, and I would have to awkwardly tell them that I had no idea. My embarrassment was the motivation I needed to seek out some answers. What I learned about my disability gave me the confidence I previously lacked when answering questions people had about my condition. What is cerebral palsy?

The part of the brain that directly affects my disability is the cerebrum, hence the term cerebral palsy. The cerebrum is responsible for controlling balance, movement, and coordination – how our muscles function together. The word palsy means uncontrollable body movement. Cerebral palsy (CP) is the term used to describe a group of brain disorders that affect a person's movement. Within that group, there is a wide variation in the degree of severity, as well as many different potential causes. Health problems in pregnant mothers can affect the baby's brain development. Damage may also result from an injury or accident that happens during pregnancy, during delivery, or shortly after.

There are different types of cerebral palsy, including spastic and non-spastic types, and the areas of the body that are affected can vary. The location of the affected areas is how the different types of CP are named:

- Monoplegia – means one affected extremity, such as an arm or leg

- Hemiplegia - means one affected side of the body, such as the left leg and left arm
- Paraplegia - typically means lower-extremity involvement
- Quadriplegia - stands for involvement of all four extremities
- Diplegia - typically means mostly lower extremity involvement, with some effect on upper extremities.

When the distribution of the affected areas and the type of CP are combined, you get the technical name for a specific diagnosis, such as spastic diplegia, which is the particular type of CP I have. The symptoms of CP can range from having a slight limp, to being wheelchair-bound, to being totally dependent on care.

People with severe cases of CP may experience involuntary movement such as waving, jerking, or extremely tight muscles. They may not be able to speak because they can't control the muscles that contribute to the act of speaking. Others may not be able to see well, or sit up. Any part of the body that muscles control can be affected. Sadly, people who don't understand the disorder may attribute the slurred speech or abnormal posture to impaired intelligence rather than a lack of muscle control. But the part of the brain that regulates cognitive skills—the cerebrum—is typically unaffected.

In my case, the left side of my body is more affected than the right, and my legs experience more difficulty than my arms.

I can move about, eat, speak, work, and live independently with the assistance of forearm crutches, but my body doesn't always do what I want it to do. At times, it can feel like my body is working against my will. My muscles try to perform the action the brain is telling them to do, but they react to the brain signal by overcompensating and tightening up all of my muscles. This makes any type of movement nearly impossible. I literally have to tell myself to relax, and once I do, my brain is able to stop sending the overwhelming signal to "do" and starts sending the signal for my muscles to "let go." As my muscles relax, I can accomplish what I set out to do.

I clearly remember one day when this was especially true, when I was twenty-two.

It was a warm summer day, and I was at a water park with friends. To make going on the rides more convenient, everyone decided to leave their shoes in a locker. Not thinking anything of it, I left my shoes behind, too. As I used my crutches to walk out onto the sun-soaked pavement, my feet felt the sting of the burning concrete, and my brain shouted, Whoa, this is hot! But instead of springing into action, moving me off the pavement, my muscles froze and held me captive in the heat. Eventually my friends glanced back when they realized I wasn't with them, and shouted: "Terra, what are you doing?!" Little did they know that I was frantically trying to follow them and escape the hot concrete, but all I could do was shout back, "I can't move!" One of my friends came back to see if I was okay, and he tried to help me by giving me his arm. But my body tightened up even more because I subconsciously try to go faster when people help me, to make it easier on them. Eventually I was able to push through and get my body to cooperate, and find some refuge in the shade. Although that was not a perfect day at the park, it is a perfect example of how my muscles sometimes do the opposite of what I want, and how my disability can hold me captive.

The heart of man plans his way, but the Lord establishes his steps.

Proverbs 16:9

CHAPTER 2

IN THE MIDDLE

I was a very active child, and one of my favorite games was being chased by my grandma. My high-pitched shrieks of excitement could often be heard throughout the house as I barreled down the hallway. I always had a trusty sidekick in my escapades. Before I used crutches, I moved with a little walker in tow. In the midst of all the fun I was having, I was unaware of all the scuff marks I was leaving behind. They lined the hallways, telling stories of my many adventures.

My walker did not, however, start out as a very appealing sidekick for a four-year-old. Its silver bars and red plastic handles were harsh and sterile until I added my personal touch, covering every inch of the bars with stickers that left hardly any shiny metal to be seen. My walker went with me everywhere. I stood in the middle of its frame, which surrounded my sides and back, and I pulled it along as I walked. It was safe, stable, sturdy, and made me feel secure. Sometimes, if there were no chairs around, I'd pop myself up onto the back bar and have my own portable, makeshift seat. My mom would often worry about the walker tipping over when I did this, but I felt confident in my space.

From preschool to third grade, my walker was my constant companion. At school, I wasn't conscious of my disability and my friends weren't either. Whether it was because of the healthy self-esteem my family and friends had helped to instill in me or because of my classmates themselves, I was treated just like everybody else, and never felt limited in what I could do. I was in a mainstream classroom at Eaton Elementary, with the only accommodation being adaptive PE, where modifications were made for me to participate in the exercises and sports. I was embraced by other kids my age; never once did I experience any bullying or rejection. During recess, I was never picked last for sports or schoolyard activities, and the kids spontaneously adapted their games so I could participate. Not once did I hear, "She can't play."

Alexandra, one of my elementary school friends, recently told me that the fact that I used a walker or a wheelchair never phased her. We didn't let it get in the way of what we wanted to do, whether we were making Spice Girls music videos, playing games at school, or swimming at one of our friends' houses. I was just part of the gang. One of my favorite memories was a day at school when my friends and I were playing in the schoolyard during recess. We were trying to recreate the environment we had seen in *The Land Before Time* by constructing paths out of the fallen leaves. I distinctly remember one classmate shouting out, "Don't forget to make the trails big enough for Terra's walker!" Everyone happily joined in without thinking twice.

Then a day came when my physical therapist recommended that I try improving my mobility by transitioning to forearm crutches. Everything about crutches was different from what I was used to. Using crutches emulated more of a "normal" walking pattern. They also required my posture to become more erect, and I was using more arm strength now than in the past. Change is never easy, and this change was especially hard for me. I was losing what kept me from my fear of falling, and it was terrifying. I was going to have to adjust to a more physically demanding and unstable form of getting around.

My walker had given me the freedom to confidently keep up with my friends on the playground. It was a source of comfort to me because I knew I could get from point A to B efficiently. Eventually, my fear of the instability that came with using my crutches faded, and I was able to gain more independence and mobility than I'd had with my walker. But it definitely was not as easy a process as that last sentence makes it sound. Something as harmless as a cotton ball on the floor became a hazard as I tried to learn this new method of maneuvering. I encountered my fair share of bumps and bruises along the way.

When I made the transition to crutches, not only did the way I moved around change; the way I was able to interact with my friends changed as well. For instance, I wasn't able to maintain my former role as one of the people who swung the jump rope around while my friends jumped. Luckily, my peers and I were at the age where we weren't as interested in jump rope or playing any more. "Talking" with each other was of more importance to us now. So I didn't have to worry: I was still part of the group.

While I was excelling socially in elementary school, I was not excelling academically. My parents were concerned that I wasn't receiving an adequate education or applying myself fully to my schoolwork. So at the start of my fifth-grade year, I was enrolled in a private school, where my class size dropped dramatically from about forty students to eight.

At this new school I faced a variety of difficulties. Aside from being the only student with a physical disability, I was the new kid on the block and was going to have to start all over at making friends. It's not that the other students shunned me, but a lot of them had known each other since kindergarten, and at this school you stayed with your classmates until you finished eighth grade. This resulted in really tight social groups. I now faced the struggle of keeping up with the new, more intense curriculum, along with the added challenge of feeling like an outsider for the first time in my life.

Even though my new classmates tried hard to make me feel welcome, and invited me to all their parties and gatherings, that sense of belonging I had felt in public school was missing. I was not feeling excluded because I had a physical disability; rather, I was putting up a wall that prevented me from connecting with these kids. I was about eleven years old at this point and had reached the time in my life where I started to care what others thought about me. I think most people can empathize with this struggle of trying to figure out where they fit in and who they are. Suddenly, the opinions of others determined my value. I hadn't worried about this before because I was confident in who I was. The core people in my life made sure I knew that I was loved, and that I felt encouraged and supported. Yet, I still was insecure. I was okay with the fact that I was disabled, but I did not expect others to be okay with it like I was.

I assumed that my classmates would not truly be my friends because my disability would make them feel uncomfortable. I thought they would pity me or simply show me kindness because of my situation, not because they saw value in me as a person. I felt the need to protect myself from the disappointment of never developing genuine relationships.

I had created a new disability for myself by being fearful of making friendships. I had built a social barrier.

This continued into high school. I found myself at another new school, feeling like I didn't fit in anywhere. The students from adaptive PE had already formed close friendships; socializing with able-bodied kids was difficult because I looked different from everybody else on the outside. I felt as though I was floating in the middle.

What I did not understand was that God had placed me in the middle for a reason. It was my friend Cristal who pointed it out to me some years later. "Terra, you have the best of both worlds," she would say to me. She explained that by having a disability, I understood the struggles that come with that life, but I could also relate to people who were able-bodied because I shared many of the same life challenges.

I know now that she was right, and that my unique point of view is a blessing. I realize that I have the ability to easily make friends, but the self-inflicted isolation I had built up during my school years was disabling me from using that gift. Little did I know that God would work through *all* of my disabilities, drawing me closer to Him, and in the process allowing Him to shine through me.

He has saved us and called us to a holy life—not because of anything we have done but because of his own purpose and grace.

2 Timothy 1:9

CHAPTER 3

TRUE HEART TRANSFORMATION

"We're going to try a little experiment today," my teacher announced. We were studying the Renaissance in my sophomore world history class, and were discussing the religious beliefs about the afterlife during that time period. The common belief was that if people were not bad enough to go straight to hell or good enough to go directly to heaven when they died, purgatory was the place they could cleanse themselves of their sins in hopes of eventually getting into heaven. To avoid purgatory, people would attempt to live a life full of good deeds in order to secure their place in heaven.

My teacher asked us to look around and write down the name of the one person in the class we thought was good enough to deserve heaven. The first person who shared her answer read my name. The second person also read my name. Sensing a pattern, my teacher asked, "Out of curiosity, how many people wrote down Terra's name?" Almost the entire class raised their hands. When asked why they had chosen me, the person who had been the first to read her response replied, "Oh, she's really nice." This puzzled me. Knowing there were other nice people in the class, I wondered if my disability had somehow influenced their opinion. I still don't fully know why so many students wrote down my name. I have a feeling that it had something to do with the common reaction of pity that I've observed when people are faced with someone with a disability.

This was not the first time I had been the recipient of pity. As long as I can remember, people have bolted to open doors for me on their own accord. I had a friend in the second grade who insisted on unpacking my lunch for me every day. Being capable of unpacking my lunch myself, I did think it was strange that she wanted to help me in this way, but I also knew that she was just trying to be nice and show that she was my friend. Once, during a trip to the mall, a store manager felt compelled to open up a separate register that allowed me to avoid standing in a long line. On several occasions, my Starbucks orders have been graciously paid for by anonymous donors. My heart is full of gratitude and thankfulness toward these acts of kindness. Yet this special treatment was subconsciously affecting how I viewed my standing with God.

When I was young, I always thought I was a good person. I obeyed my parents and rarely found myself in trouble. While I did not grow up going to church, and neither of my parents were religious, I would occasionally attend church with my friends and their families. These infrequent Sunday school lessons and the well-intentioned words of people telling me how much God loved me were all that comprised my limited knowledge of God. I grew up in a happy little bubble, somehow acquiring the idea that having cerebral palsy made me *more* special than others in God's eyes. *Yeah, that's right, God loves me. I'm good.*

By the time I got to college, I was on the verge of developing a huge *spiritual ego*.

The gravity of sin never crossed my mind. I was a relatively "good person" because I did not fall into the typical struggles of most young college students. I didn't really care if I sinned; I thought that God would consider my sin less weighty because I had a disability. I just assumed I would be going to heaven—as if I had a free pass.

At that time I was sporadically attending The Well Community Church in Fresno with a group of friends. I only went because I thought that's what Christians were supposed to do. 1 Corinthians 2:14 says: "The person without the Spirit does not accept the things that come from the Spirit of God but considers them foolishness, and cannot understand them because they are discerned only through the Spirit." That was me! Because my heart had not been transformed by Christ, the sermons, which taught the opposite of what the world says, were difficult for me to grasp.

I believed there was a God from what I had soaked up as a child attending Sunday school with friends. But just believing that God exists is not enough; your response is what ultimately matters. James 2:19: says, "You believe that there is one God. Good! Even the demons believe that—and shudder." The demons believe in God, and their response is to quake in fear. Satan believes in God, but his response is to rebel against Him out of pride and envy. Belief in God does not equal love for God.

At this point I didn't have a relationship with Him and did not care about giving my life to Him. I hadn't made the decision to accept Him as my Lord and Savior. I hadn't asked Jesus for forgiveness of my sins, and therefore wasn't yet reconciled to God by the blood of Christ—meaning, my relationship with God had not yet been restored. I was only projecting the *image* of someone who was living a life for God, without having to be accountable for any of my decisions. I was spiritually disabled.

But I was starting to become tired of trying to look like a *Christian* on the outside, knowing that this was a facade. I tried to act like a good person and treated others well to their faces, even if five minutes later I was tearing them down with things I would say about them behind their backs. Yeah, I went to church, but maybe once every three months. I bought into the lie that attending church was what gave me the right to call myself a Christian. The life I was living felt empty, like I was missing something. I was twenty-two when this restlessness started. I remember walking around downtown Santa Cruz, California, with my long time group of friends, the same friends I attended The Well with. These were the people who knew me inside and out, people I considered to be family. I had always felt secure when with them, and yet I remember feeling this deep sense of longing for something more starting to creep in. I felt stuck in a superficial life, living solely for myself, while the people closest to me did the same. My sense of fulfillment couldn't be found in these relationships anymore. I didn't know it yet, but I was longing for Christ. That's when the Lord stepped in. As I window-shopped, I wondered if it would always be like this. To my astonishment, God whispered to my heart and told me, *It won't always be like this because you are going to follow me.*

As with most change, following God did not happen instantly, but as time went on, I could not shake the longing I felt to live for something greater. I desired to have purpose, but was unsure what my calling was. Even knowing God's promise, I kept it to myself. But God pursued me even so. Rebecca Faires writes in her *She Reads Truth* Lenten study, "Ephesians tells us 'we are His creation, created in Christ Jesus for good works, which God prepared ahead of time so that we should walk in them' (Ephesians 2:10). We can't escape God and His stormy gale of purpose. He pursues us with love that is filled with a beautiful intensity unlike anything else we have ever known."

He led me to a small, multicultural church called I.S.I. Ministries in Fresno. The sense of fellowship in this body of believers was strong, and the people were genuine. I.S.I. stands for "Iron Sharpens Iron," which is taken from Proverbs 27:17: "Iron sharpens iron, and one man sharpens another." It didn't take long for me to realize, *Wow, these people really do love God.*

Before coming to this church, my mindset was that my obligations came before church, which was an extracurricular activity. These people, by contrast, lived in a manner that prioritized God over worldly responsibilities. They understood that He is more important than anything else in this world. They made sure they were active participants in the church despite everything that was going on in their lives. They held praise and worship nights on Fridays, took time to prepare and send care packages to former members who were attending school out of town, and valued praying with and for each other. Members were intentional about holding each other accountable, studying the word together, and showing others love by meeting whatever needs they had.

These people not only heard the word, but actually did what it said. This was the exact opposite of what I had experienced in my group of friends. The members of this church lived up to the Scripture their ministry was named after. It was so new and intriguing to me that I kept coming back. This little ministry is where my faith really started to grow.

I felt like I went through something similar to what happened to Saul, the way things changed: "And immediately something like scales fell from his eyes, and he regained his sight…" (Acts 9:18). It wasn't so much that this church was different from anything I'd been to before; rather, my heart was responding to the promptings of the Holy Spirit. There wasn't a specific sermon that stood out to me or changed my life, but through both the teaching I received at this church and studying God's word on my own, I distinctly remember becoming aware of God's holiness for the first time.

I gained a clear understanding that my impatience, judgmental tendencies, hurtful gossip, and proclivity for being self-centered actually mattered in God's eyes. I was dead in my sin and needed a Savior. I had prayed once before, in sixth grade, for Christ to come into my heart after watching a Christmas program at a local church, not really knowing or caring what that meant. Eleven years later, I prayed this prayer again. This time, instead of just accepting Christ, I was surrendering my life to Him. I wanted Him to change my life from the inside out and to live out whatever purpose He had for me. This time, my heart was truly transformed.

After this huge change in my spiritual life, people around me started to notice and tell me I was different. My focus was turned from myself, knowing that I was truly loved by God despite my flaws, and my purpose was to let my life be a reflection of His love. My friends wondered why I spent so much time at church, and others around me began to make comments regarding my newfound joy. My friend Alyssa says that it's as if I have tiny holes all over my body, the size of straws, and through each hole shines a light from within. This is evidence that I now have a genuine faith, and I believe that God has given me this gift of joy. Even though I don't always feel like being joyful, He still provides it. My hope is in Jesus, not in people or my circumstances, and that is why my joy can be constant.

My disability helps me point people to Jesus because I lean on Him every day. Cerebral palsy is not my free pass; it is what draws me close to my Savior. Cerebral palsy allows me to say, "I can do everything through him who gives me strength" (Philippians 4:13).

Looking back through my life thus far, I see how God planted seeds throughout my childhood, even when attending church was an obligation rather than an opportunity to learn. Because of this, my faith was able to come to fruition.

The midcentury Evangelical author Arthur Pink wrote: "Our lives are neither the product of blind fate nor the result of capricious chance, but every detail of them was ordained from all eternity, and is now ordered by the living and reigning God."

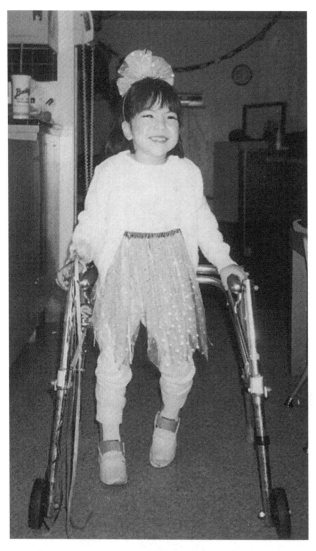

My elementary school days - all dressed up cruising around in my walker.

Dad and I in Disneyland.

Touring the Taj Mahal in 2012 with BTB.

Rappelling off a 60ft. bridge in South Africa with BTB.

With my fellow BTB teammates after the 2017 CityFest Performance in Fresno, CA, featuring the singers from For King and Country.

My friend Rachael and I never pass up an opportunity to eat ice cream!

My last day in Peru with BTB after giving my wheelchair to Will.

Hanging out with my family!

Decked out in my Halloween costume, hanging out with some of my favorite little friends.

One of the Maids of Honor in my friend, Nathalia's wedding!

A snapshot from my last performance in Guatemala with BTB.

For I know that nothing good dwells in me, that is, in my flesh. For I have the desire to do what is right, but not the ability to carry it out.

Romans 7:18

CHAPTER 4

SPIRITUALLY DISABLED

As I started attending church and intentionally spending time in God's presence and studying His word, I began to grow in my knowledge of the Lord. I learned through the Book of Romans that in God's eyes, sin is sin (Romans 3:9-10, 3:23.) It's widely understood that killing someone has greater repercussions than stealing a box of chocolates. God established appropriate punishment for each sin. Even though the actions result in different consequences, however, the root of the sin is still the same. Both the person who stole the chocolates and the one convicted of murder chose to put their own interests above all else. No matter how the action presents itself, when you choose to sin, you are putting yourself before God. James 2:10 says: "For whoever keeps the whole law but fails in one point has become guilty of all of it."

Because God is holy, He can't be near sin at all. Therefore, if there is any degree of sin in us, it separates us from His presence. In Scripture I read that there is no such thing as a righteous person; we all sin and fail to meet God's standards of perfect holiness. I came to understand that when the Bible says *all*, that includes me.

I became aware of my sins. I was afflicted with deep matters of the heart. I was gossiping, judging others, and wrestling with pride. These sins were separating me from a relationship with God and preventing me from putting Him as the Lord of my life. Since no one was able to see these internal sins, it was easier to pretend that everything was fine, even though inside I was fearful that others might see what was really going on. But God can see right through a deceptive heart. Even if the entire world wanted to show me pity because I have cerebral palsy, that *still* would not get me any closer to God or Heaven.

God cares about the condition of my soul, not the opinions of others. The world's standards have no comparison to the Lord's standards. The Bible tells us that His ways are higher than ours (Isaiah 55:8-10). I am a flawed human being and cannot live up to God's standard of good. Since everyone is flawed, no one has the ability to save themselves from their sin and depravity. This puts us all on a level playing field: we are all spiritually disabled.

Disability is not exclusively limited to physical or mental shortcomings. Some of the most crippling disabilities are those that impact one emotionally or spiritually. People might assume cerebral palsy makes me weak, but I feel my greatest hindrance is my pride. Just like cerebral palsy makes it more difficult for me to go about daily tasks, my pride makes it much more difficult for me to daily give up what I selfishly want and follow Christ instead.

I believe, from what I've read in the Bible, that pride is at the root of all sin. God hates pride because we really have a misplaced sense of worth. God says that "In his pride the wicked man does not seek him; in all his thoughts there is no room for God" (Psalm 10:4).

I struggle with the constant desire to be in control of my life, and I think the fact that I don't always have control over my own body plays a large part in my desire to control. If I can control the situations I find myself in, I feel more comfortable. I do not trust the plans He has for me and find it difficult to submit my future to Him. I think I can handle my life better than the one who created me and has already mapped out every detail of my life. With this ongoing battle of not being able to put my full trust in God, my lack of control makes me fearful, and I worry about the end result. I always want *what I want*, thinking that God has something lesser for me, even though Romans 8:28 refutes that by saying, "we know that for those who love God all things work together for good, for those who are called according to his purpose."

Not only do I not always trust God, but when people do me wrong or hurt me, I want to cut them out of my life. My pride causes me to care only about myself, not about the other persons involved or how my actions will affect them. I'd rather protect myself than continue to be a true friend and be there to bear their burdens. So I avoid them, talk badly about them, and when I do come in contact with them, I make sure they know by my demeanor that I want nothing to do with them.

Ironically, I expect God to continue showing grace and mercy to me, even though I don't want to show them grace or mercy. Because they inflicted pain, my pride rears its ugly head and convinces me that somehow their sin against me is greater than my sins against God. My pride drives me to maintain control of the outcome of the situation because I want to make sure it works out in favor of my comfort, what I believe I deserve.

This struggle with pride is not just exclusive to me; the battle for control between God and humans is an age-old dispute. Since the beginning, we have struggled with pride. C.S. Lewis describes pride as "...wanting to be the centre...wanting to be God...." Adam and Eve exhibited this when they chose to deliberately disobey God's command in the garden. Even before they chose to eat the fruit from the tree, Satan was kicked out of heaven for this very sin. It is ultimately pride that separated creation from the Creator, therefore making it the ultimate disability. Since we, as humans, separated ourselves from God through sin, He had to overcome this disability by sending His son to die in our place.

It is the grace He showed through this act that compels me to live for Him. Now that I truly understand the price of this grace and the magnitude of His love for my sinful self, I see how undeserving I really am. The reality of this gift results in a gratitude that is lived out through service, allowing me to use my talent to make an impact for His Kingdom.

*But be sure to fear the Lord and serve him faithfully
with all your heart; consider what great things he
has done for you.*

1 Samuel 12:24

CHAPTER 5

STRENGTH IN WEAKNESS

We can talk about inclusion all we want, but unless you know what it looks like, it's hard to live it. Fortunately, I've had the privilege of experiencing the benefits of inclusion my whole life. When I was four years old, a friend of my parents recommended that I try getting involved with a nonprofit organization in Fresno called Break the Barriers (BTB). BTB was founded by Steve and Deby Hergenrader in 1983 because of Deby's sister Kathy, who had Down syndrome. Growing up, Kathy was not allowed to participate in the same sports activities as Deby because of the ignorance

51

and stigma associated with disability. Driven by their desire for everyone to be given a chance, this couple created something that is one of a kind.

BTB is not only a place where people with disabilities can take classes in different types of sports and art forms, but also where they can be part of a performing team. This team shares the message that you don't have to be limited by your physical, mental, or circumstantial state; you have purpose and worth no matter what label you've been given by society. The presentations resemble something you might see during a Cirque du Soleil performance. The team travels all over the world to spread the word to as many people as possible. This is the outlet that God provided me with to share my faith, serve others, and be an encouragement.

This group is composed of all kinds of talented athletes. Some are accomplished gymnasts, dancers, and martial artists. Others are also talented athletes who happen to have a physical or mental disability of some kind. The team showcases what these athletes can do when people are not confined by what society says they should be able to do. For instance, during a performance, one might see a person with spina bifida standing on his head while strapped to his wheelchair, an individual who has Down syndrome holding a gymnast on his shoulders, or a gymnast who only has one arm being tossed through the center of a hula hoop. When I was on the team, my role was as a dancer on wheels, meaning that I danced while in my wheelchair. My teammates would figure out how to incorporate me into a trick, such as a handstand on the wheelchair, while I would spin both of us in a circle. (See the YouTube video at https://www.youtube.com/user/btb4all for some footage from our performances.)

The performances serve as a visual illustration of inclusion and how beautiful various abilities working together can be. Having been on this team for so many years and seeing all the amazing tricks that can be accomplished, I feel the term disability does not apply with this group. "We all have abilities and disabilities. If we don't think we have a disability now, disabilities will come with old age. We have to look beyond what we think we see, because inside is ability," Deby says.

Surprisingly, it is not necessarily our performances that touch people's hearts, no matter how inspiring they may be. Both at home and around the world, we have seen that what touches people the most is the way the teammates interact with each other. Every member of the team cares for each other like a family. My teammates would never have treated me like someone who is helpless or incapable. They expected the same from me that they would expect from anyone else, and if I had trouble with something, they helped me figure out a way to accomplish it.

Sometimes while traveling in other countries, we would find ourselves in places where there were no elevators, which made getting to the second floor nearly impossible for those of us who used wheelchairs. If a team member was unable to walk up stairs, two able-bodied teammates would carry that person up the stairs in his or her chair. Personally, I am able to climb up and down stairs with someone's assistance or by using handrails if they are available. There was always a teammate ready to assist me by holding onto my arm or carrying my chair up behind me.

Other times we found ourselves in situations where we needed to board our flight quickly, and our gate was all the way across the airport. Rather than waiting for the elevator, the team would all hop on the escalator together (yes, *all*, including those who used wheelchairs). A teammate would come up behind me and pop my wheelchair back, so that the front wheels would be propped up on one step and the back of the chair would be propped up against the teammate's leg on the step below. We always turned a lot of heads when doing this, and most of the time, we received looks of amazement or amusement. But there were also many instances where we would receive a frown of disapproval and a finger wag from a security guard. Then we would have to get off and frantically try to find the nearest elevator, crossing our fingers that we wouldn't miss our flight. But nobody on the team gives up if the circumstances look impossible at first glance. The team is ready to modify and improvise no matter what the situation is.

With this team I traveled to Romania, China, South Africa, the Dominican Republic, India, Australia, Peru, the Philippines, and Guatemala. Throughout our travels, we constantly encountered the misconception that disability is a curse that is a result of God's punishment. Even among religious people here in the United States, the idea that disability is a by-product of living in a fallen, sinful world is not uncommon. Nor is the belief that disability is the result of an unfortunate mistake. Yet God's word contradicts the idea that disability is a curse, a mistake, or a punishment.

Just as many people do today, Jesus's disciples had the same question, two thousand years ago. "As [Jesus] passed by, he saw a man blind from birth. And his disciples asked him, 'Rabbi, who sinned, this man or his parents, that he was born blind?' Jesus answered, 'It was not that this man sinned, or his parents, but that the works of God might be displayed in him'" (John 9). At the time, there was a cultural belief that righteousness and holiness were rewarded with health, wealth, and prosperity. So people assumed that if you were poor or sick, it was due to your sin or your family's. Jesus explains to his disciples that the disability was not punishment for sins, but rather, that God would be glorified through our weakness (2 Corinthians 12:7-10).

God often chooses to use unlikely people to make an impact for his kingdom. Stories of people who seem *underqualified* to do God's work are intertwined throughout the Bible. Moses struggled with a speech impediment, but God chose him to be His spokesperson, to tell the Pharaoh of Egypt to free the people of Israel from slavery. David was a simple shepherd boy who didn't even cross his father's mind when God sent Samuel to anoint one of his sons as king, but God chose David to rule over the nation of Israel. Mary was just a young girl from a small, despised town who did not possess a royal pedigree, yet God chose her to give birth to the King of the world.

I know I don't necessarily look like the type of person that people expect God to use, since the world sees me as someone who may need to rely on the help of others when it comes to doing everyday tasks. "But God chose what is foolish in the world to shame the wise; God chose what is weak in the world to shame the strong" (1 Corinthians 1:27).

I have found that my disability is the tool that God uses to minister to others. I saw this play out firsthand during my time spent in Cusco, Peru. My team and I had the opportunity to visit a hospital that was also home for several children and young adults with various physical disabilities. Some lived there because they needed ongoing treatment. Others had been left there because their families did not have the financial stability to maintain proper care for them. While we were visiting with the patients, one young man excitedly began to motion toward my wheelchair, which I used for performances.

"How do I get a chair like yours?"

I had to pull the translator over, as I couldn't understand what he was saying. As I wheeled myself back a bit, I could see why he was so frantic. This young man was sitting in a wheelchair that didn't fit him. It was too big. His arms could not reach over the armrests because the wheels were set out too wide, which prevented him from having full range of motion to correctly maneuver the chair. Having a wheelchair that does not fit is like wearing a shoe that does not fit. When a wheelchair is your main mode of transportation, it has to fit correctly in order for you to go about your day. I sat and listened to his story. His name was Will. This young man was in a terrible bicycle accident, resulting in paralysis from the waist down.

"Do you want to try out my chair?" I asked him.

It was amazing! A chair that was customized specifically for me seemed to fit this young man just as well, with only a few makeshift adjustments. I watched him as he maneuvered my chair around with ease. Everyone could see it was like night and day comparing the two chairs. Just being able to turn in a circle without issue made Will beam with joy.

"Give him your chair," God impressed upon my heart, as I sat and watched him enjoying himself. With the help of my medical insurance, I knew I would be able to order another chair when I arrived home. We happened to be flying home in just a few hours. I would not need it on the trip anymore, since we had finished performing and I had my crutches to get around with. I turned to Julia, one of the Peruvian missionaries we had partnered with, and said, "I want to give him my chair.

Knowing that this costly gift should not be taken lightly, she told me that I should hold him to a few contingencies upon receiving this gift of mobility. The first was that he must reenroll in the local university to pursue a degree. The second was that he continue applying himself at physical therapy, to keep building muscle and improving his overall health. She wanted him to be a good steward of this gift, and not waste the independence and opportunities that having this chair would give him.

Through the translator, I told Will, "I want to give you my chair, because everything I have ultimately comes from God and is not mine to hold on to. I want to make your life easier." I then listed the contingencies that came with this gift.

As the translator relayed what I had said, Will gave me a hug and excitedly thanked me, ready to keep exploring what he could do in this chair that afforded him a freedom he had not known since his accident.

A few months after we arrived home from Peru, I received a Facebook message from Will. He had discovered how much a chair like mine was worth, and tried to communicate to me how grateful he was and how much of an impact my gift had made on him. Because the message was not translated well over the internet, I reached out to Julia to understand what he was attempting to tell me. She told me that when he found out the cost of my gift, he called her in tears. He could not believe that someone would give away something so valuable. She told him that I had been able to gift him my chair so easily because it was the love of God that had prompted me to do so. She also told him that even though he had been blessed immensely by my gift, that it blessed me as well, knowing that my obedience had made such a difference in the quality of his life.

I later found out that Will had, in fact, committed to his physical therapy, and had enrolled in school again. He was so serious about fulfilling the things he had promised to me that when he was unable to catch a taxi to school, he would wheel the two-mile journey to ensure he made it to class. That told me he was truly dedicated to his education.

In addition to God using me to bless others on our trips, I have been blessed with an abundance of life-changing experiences. I have witnessed God use the team to influence the Congress of Guatemala to revisit the Disability Acts that had been neglected for years because they were deemed unimportant. In South Africa, an eighteen-year-old woman who had been paralyzed in a skiing accident was inspired to try to walk again after seeing the team perform. In Peru, the team was there to lift up a woman as she fell to her knees and asked Jesus to be her Lord and Savior. This was after her pastor had told her that her son's cerebral palsy was God's way of punishing her for her past sins. It is difficult to put into words how overwhelmingly humbled I feel to have these memories to reflect on. What a privilege it has been to serve God in this way!

*For we are his workmanship, created in Christ Jesus
for good works, which God prepared beforehand,
that we should walk in them.*

Ephesians 2:10

CHAPTER 6

OPPORTUNITY

God used me and my disability to reach Will in a
way that the rest of my teammates could not. The act
of giving away my chair was a visible representation
of the selfless love of Christ. Having this opportunity
to help meet one of Will's needs affirmed my belief
that every individual, regardless of ability level, has a
unique, God-ordained purpose. My time on the Barrier
Breaker team was merely one of the many purposes I
believe God has for me. On these mission trips, I was
able to show that every individual life is important,
and that God works through all of His children, not
just the seemingly capable ones. First Corinthians
echoes this sentiment and compares the church to a

human body, describing how each part or member is necessary for the body to work as a cohesive whole.

I believe that this concept applies to our world as well, *and that each individual has a unique role to fill.*

For the body does not consist of one member but of many. If the foot should say, "Because I am not a hand, I do not belong to the body," that would not make it any less a part of the body. And if the ear should say, "Because I am not an eye, I do not belong to the body," that would not make it any less a part of the body. If the whole body were an eye, where would be the sense of hearing? If the whole body were an ear, where would be the sense of smell? But as it is, God arranged the members in the body, each one of them, as he chose. If all were a single member, where would the body be? As it is, there are many parts, yet one body. The eye cannot say to the hand, "I have no need of you," nor again the head to the feet, "I have no need of you." On the contrary, the parts of the body that seem to be weaker are indispensable, and on those parts of the body that we think less honorable we bestow the greater honor, and our unpresentable parts are treated with greater modesty, which our more presentable parts do not require. But God has so composed the body, giving greater honor to the part that lacked it, that there may be no division in the body, but that the members may have the same care for one another. (1 Corinthians 12:14-25)

As verse 22 states, even "the parts of the body that seem to be weaker are indispensable." It is time the Church applied this to their members with disabilities. Even though these congregants may appear weak or incapable, they have a vital purpose in this world.

I have a young friend named Alli who has cerebral palsy, is blind, and is wheelchairbound. She has very limited use of her arms and legs, does not communicate verbally, and is dependent on others for all daily tasks. When people look at her, they may see someone who is dispensable, but I know that is not true. I have seen how even with her limited physical ability, she has the power to reach hearts with just her smile and laugh. She is not full of misery, by any means; this girl loves her life! She is one of the happiest people I know, and I have seen her gifts at work firsthand.

One day when we were together in Sunday school, a substitute leader who did not know her seemed as if he had already written her off in his mind as a student who was not worth pouring time and effort into. This could have been because he was intimidated by her differences, inability to communicate in traditional ways, or maybe he assumed she could not comprehend what was going on. But as the other children shared funny stories, and she was being her upbeat self and laughing in response to their silliness, I could see his heart melt as he recognized her beautiful spirit. From that point on, he was drawn to her. I could tell that he really saw *her* instead of just a girl in a wheelchair. Despite being totally dependent on others for her physical care, she is able to point others to the Creator with the gift of joy He has given her. This is her purpose in our church body.

I may have to do things differently because of my disability, but that doesn't diminish my life's worth. My value does not come from my external qualities or characteristics, but from my soul and how I live my life; and these things come from God. While it's true that I do experience some challenges in day-to-day life, it's minimal in comparison with what my life would be like without Christ. A quote I read in *Disability and the Sovereign Goodness of God* by John Piper, the pastor of Bethlehem Baptist Church in Bethlehem, Pennsylvania, resonated with me. In this book, Piper includes a portion of the vision statement that Bob Horning and John Knight, both fathers of children with disabilities, wrote for the disability ministry at Bethlehem Baptist Church: "life with a disability and with Jesus is infinitely better than a healthy body without Him." God has shown me that my life has meaning and purpose, despite the difficulties I experience. Even if I were able-bodied and could walk unaided, that gift of total mobility could still never satisfy me completely. My physical limitations do not separate me from true fulfillment; my sin does.

But because of Christ's sacrifice on the cross, God allows us to serve Him and chooses to use us to accomplish His work, despite our flawed human nature. And since everyone is flawed, there is no such thing as a person who is better suited to serve God. He does not expect less from someone who experiences a physical or mental hardship. He has created all lives with a purpose, and that purpose is to further His kingdom.

No matter what disabilities we have, we should still be contributing to His work here on earth. Oftentimes in the Church, those with disabilities are praised for merely being present. I have a few friends who either experience a disability themselves or have a family member who does, and who have said that the impression they sometimes receive from well-intentioned churchgoers is that just showing up is more than enough. People should not accept someone's presence at church as good enough without contribution.

The Church is a place for us to learn, grow, repent, and build community with other believers. Most important, it equips us with a platform to serve. If there is no platform available for believers who may not be viewed as capable, we are hindering them from obedience to Christ, and ultimately, from experiencing the beauty of what God fully intended the Church to be.

Romans 12:4-8 shows us that every part of the body has a distinct role that is of great importance in accomplishing His work:

For as in one body we have many members, and the members do not all have the same function, so we, though many, are one body in Christ, and individually members one of another. Having gifts that differ according to the grace given to us, let us use them: if prophecy, in proportion to our faith; if service, in our serving; the one who teaches, in his teaching; the one who exhorts, in his exhortation; the one who contributes, in generosity; the one who leads, with zeal; the one who does acts of mercy, with cheerfulness.

It is a beautiful thing when the body of Christ works together as it should. Since God has given everyone different gifts, it would be senseless to have everyone serve in the same capacity. Where someone is not gifted, another is strong. This does not mean some gifts are better than others; it is by His grace alone that we received these gifts to use at all. All gifts are specifically given to each individual according to His sovereignty and divine plan.

Because she grew up with a sister who had Down syndrome, Deby Hergenrader was able to recognize the need for everyone to fulfill their purpose, as well as the need for circumstances that can make this a reality. "Around the world, parents are the same, they're saying the same prayer; they want a place where their child can develop the gifts that they have been given," she says."But there is lack of opportunity to do that." What better place to spark this movement than in the Church?

People who experience a disability can serve in any capacity in which their gifts are being used. The Church should not feel the need to create special areas of service for members who may seem less capable than your average church volunteer. Any member can serve in any way despite limitations, as long as adaptations are made to allow each member to be efficient in serving. Aim to give everyone the opportunity to be valuable.

Find a way to set people up for success, allowing them to use their gifts and talents to the fullest for the Lord. One of the best ways to ensure that everyone has the chance to contribute is to model *inclusion* over *integration* within the Church, or any social setting. Although the two terms sound similar, there are distinct differences. Integration is when you are part of a group, but not necessarily contributing to it, as when you are invited to a church event, but are there merely as a spectator. Inclusion, by contrast, is when each member is an integral part of the group. You are not only present in the mix, but able to meaningfully participate. Inclusion does not happen overnight; it is a lifestyle to learn. This may require an examination of what your church believes inclusion looks like.

When striving for inclusion, you cannot expect the same method to work for all individuals. We all have different personalities, needs, and skills.

For example, if my church were planning a fundraiser dinner to send other church members on a mission trip, cooking the meal for the event would not be the most efficient way for me to help. Although cooking is something I am able to do, it is difficult for me to hold objects and move about, or even to just stand for long periods of time while using my crutches. Even using my wheelchair, trying to figure out an effective way to complete the task at hand, would be a time-consuming process. It would be more productive for me to be sitting down, helping to roll silverware, for example. Or I could even help serve the food if someone pushed my wheelchair for me so my hands would be free.

There are innumerable other ways to adapt or modify service. For example, anyone can be a greeter, lead a Bible study, or be a part of a prayer group, as long as they are capable of performing the task well. Someone who is deaf can greet others before a church service starts, while simultaneously teaching people who are hearing how to sign. If people have the use of their hands, they can pass the offering plate—or set it on their lap if they use a wheelchair. Anyone can help in the coffee bar, making sure it's stocked with cups, sugar packets, etc. Those with musical talent can be a part of the worship team, if the stage is accessible. It is time to stop the pity and allow all people to do what God created them to do.

From him the whole body, joined and held together by every supporting ligament, grows and builds itself up in love, as each part does its work.

Ephesians 4:16

CHAPTER 7

A CALL TO CHANGE

Maybe with everything you have read up to now, you might see a need within your own church to invite people who experience a disability to get plugged in and serve. Maybe you know of someone who is disabled who has never had the opportunity to learn who Jesus is or to hear the Gospel. Here are some steps you can take:

1. Be a friend. As simple as this sounds, it is often very difficult, especially if you feel you have nothing in common with the other person. As a Christian, I believe in the call to "love your neighbor." In a sermon that Pastor Dave Gibbons of New Song Church in Santa Ana, California, gave when discussing Jesus's commandment to love our neighbor, he brought up the question of how we define who our neighbor is. Contrary to what many megachurches preach, he says, your *neighbor* is not necessarily someone just like you. "It's actually the exact opposite of what we've been taught," he says. "It's someone not like you. In fact, it may be somebody you even hate, and can't stand to be around." To be a good neighbor, or friend, we should love not only those who are easy to love because they are like us, but others who are outside of our comfort zone. If a person with a disability is outside of your typical comfort zone, stretching yourself to be that person's friend will not only make a difference in his or her life, but in yours as well.

2. Equip the church to meet the physical needs of your churchgoers. Catering to people's physical needs can take many different forms, including ensuring that your church is an accessible building, and providing properly trained staff as well as programs that can adapt to the needs of each family or individual with a disability. Friends of mine have been left out of church activities because the proper tools were not available, such as a wheelchair lift or a sign language interpreter for someone who is deaf. This saddens me. Being able to attend church to worship and learn with other believers is an integral part of Christianity. It should be accessible to everyone.

Over the last few years, however, I have noticed a shift toward accessibility in my community. Churches in the Fresno area are starting to ensure that their facilities can accommodate all people.

These churches are making sure the buildings are up to code with the Americans with Disabilities Act, putting in ramps, elevators, accessible seating, and parking spaces for the handicapped. Not all of these resources were available despite the ADA, and it was preventing the disabled population from attending church.

If people with disabilities cannot even get inside the building or go where they need to go on the church campus, they are missing out on the opportunity to grow and learn about God. If there are no staff members trained to work with those who need more assistance, these individuals and their families may end up leaving the church because they are not receiving the support they need. I know of a family with two boys, both on the autism spectrum, whose church was intentional about providing a special buddy system to meet their needs. But the staff members were not properly trained to work with autistic children, and the mom kept having to be called in to restore order because the buddies could not keep the students on track. That family eventually left the church because they felt like a burden.

To prevent a similar scenario from happening in your church, seek out proper training for your current staff, or consider hiring someone who specializes in a particular field, such as autism, to ensure that this ongoing need is met. Some positions to consider would be American Sign Language interpreters, staff who are trained to work with people on the autism spectrum, and aides or "buddies" for those who may need a little more assistance.

These specially trained staff members are crucial, not only to give the children an opportunity to learn about Christ, but also to give their parents some much-needed rest. It is more than likely that these parents are distracted from Christ's message because they may be constantly worrying about their medically fragile child, or are repeatedly being called into the classroom to stop their child's disruptive behavior. Many families with members who are affected by a disability do not even attend church because they feel like an inconvenience. It may be an embarrassing experience because their child or family member is different, and there may not be anyone in the church who has the knowledge and desire to work with them. So to avoid being judged for their child's actions, it is easier for them to simply not attend.

These families need to have a time to refuel and be in community with other believers, just like any other family. Most almost never get a break, as they are constantly caring for their child's needs and often the sibling's as well. It is vital that their walk with Christ is strengthened so they can keep going. To ensure that families like this are not left out, be intentional in praying for God to bring the right staff to your church. Make inclusion so much a part of your church culture that your congregation simply expects it.

3. Find a way to plug those who are disabled into the current serving opportunities in your church.

I have a nineteen-year-old friend named Zach who happens to have Down syndrome. He has preached sermons at his church and is part of a co-ed Bible study. Zach is known and loved by those who attend. He sometimes needs a little help finding the right passage, but he is there with his Bible open, sharing prayer requests.

His heart for the Lord is evident, and he touches those around him just by being himself. For example, an acquaintance with a physical disability confided to Zach how he struggles to make friends. He told Zach that he felt as though people don't see him as a person; they just see his chair. Zach prayed for him and let him know that there was someone who wanted to be his friend, and that was Jesus. A few weeks later, the student told Zach that he wanted to meet Jesus.

Zach was not meant to be praising Jesus from the sidelines, simply because he has Down syndrome. He has a specific set of gifts: to be a mover and shaker for God's kingdom.

I hope every church takes a page from Zach's story and finds ways to use every member of the body by discovering their abilities and allowing them to contribute. Zach once said, "My calling is to tell other people with disabilities about Jesus." It's up to us to ensure that callings can become a reality for people like Zach and myself.

4. If you are not in a position to influence church policy, you may not be able to effect these changes. But something everyone can do to live with a sense of inclusion is to not avoid the topic of disability.

The next time someone asks you, "What happened to her?," be honest, straightforward, and just talk about it. Disability is not something to be ashamed of. Avoiding the question merely breeds mystery, which often leads to fear. I am always willing and happy to share my story, and I have found that the majority of people I know who experience a disability generally feel the same.

I do not think I will ever stop hearing that question, "Mom, what happened to her?" Through this book, however, I hope I have exposed misconceptions about disability, and inspired readers to take action and bring about positive change in how the Church views disability. Both as individuals and as the Church body, we must ensure that all believers have the opportunity and the tools to fulfill the purpose that God has designed them for. In doing this, we are not only being obedient, but making the Church what God originally intended it to be.

I want to abolish the fear, avoidance, and pity that so many seem to have toward disability. Because of my belief that God has created me like this for a reason, I have never thought that my life was not fair. Even before my faith was strong, I never felt that my situation was unjust, but have always had a contented heart toward my disability. It is part of who I am. I do not dwell on the fact that I have cerebral palsy; instead, I pour my time and energy into things that are important to me and matter beyond this lifetime. I would not choose to have a normally functioning body for one second, because I firmly believe that disability and I work together for one purpose, and that is to glorify God.

I understand that this contentment is not prevalent in everyone who experiences some sort of disability. I can see God's hand throughout my entire life and His loving kindness placing me in environments in which I was protected, accepted, and loved. But I know a lot of people who, because of their condition, experience chronic pain or have been bullied. Some may have had their mobility taken from them as the result of an accident or sickness, and now struggle with the loss of their former way of life and their dreams for their future. I in no way want to diminish the hardships associated with disability. Instead, it is my sincere desire that if you find yourself navigating through this kind of pain or the "Why, God?" moments, that you truly understand you have a God-ordained purpose in your affliction. He is a God who creates "beauty from ashes," and redeems the brokenness in this world caused by sin. (Isaiah 61:3)

I hope I have given you positive insight on what it's like to live a life using the gifts He has given for the benefit of others, despite having a disability. It is my intention that all of us feel encouraged to serve, regardless of our shortcomings, and to help ensure that everyone has an opportunity to serve no matter their situation. My challenge to you is to live out the command in 1 Peter 4:10: "Each one should use whatever gift he has received to serve others, faithfully administering God's grace in its various forms."

Citations and Sources

Biblical

And he said to them, "Follow me, and I will make you fishers of men." Matthew 4:19 ESV

For you formed my inward parts; you knitted me together in my mother's womb. I praise you, for I am fearfully and wonderfully made. Wonderful are your works;my soul knows it very well. My frame was not hidden from you, when I was being made in secret, intricately woven in the depths of the earth. Your eyes saw my unformed substance; in your book were written, every one of them, the days that were formed for me, when as yet there was none of them. Psalm 139:13-16 ESV

The heart of man plans his way, but the Lord establishes his steps. Proverbs 16:9 ESV

He has saved us and called us to a holy life—not because of anything we have done but because of his own purpose and grace. 2 Timothy 1:9 NIV

The person without the Spirit does not accept the things that come from the Spirit of God but considers them foolishness, and cannot understand them because they are discerned only through the Spirit. 1 Corinthians 2:14 NIV

You believe that there is one God. Good! Even the demons believe that—and shudder. James 2:19 NIV

For we are His workmanship, created in Christ Jesus for good works, which God prepared beforehand that we should walk in them. Ephesians 2:10 NKJV

As iron sharpens iron, so one person sharpens another. Proverbs 27:17 NIV

And immediately something like scales fell from his eyes, and he regained his sight. Then he rose and was baptized. Acts 9:18 ESV

I can do all this through him who gives me strength. Philippians 4:13 NIV

For I know that nothing good dwells in me, that is, in my flesh. For I have the desire to do what is right, but not the ability to carry it out. Romans 7:18 ESV

For whoever keeps the whole law but fails in one point has become guilty of all of it. James 2:10 ESV

What then? Are we Jews any better off? No, not at all. For we have already charged that all, both Jews and Greeks, are under sin, as it is written: "None is righteous, no, not one." Romans 3:9-10 ESV

For all have sinned and fall short of the glory of God. Romans 3:23 ESV

In his pride the wicked man does not seek him; in all his thoughts there is no room for God. Psalm 10:4 NIV

And we know that for those who love God all things work together for good, for those who are called according to his purpose. Romans 8:28 ESV

For my thoughts are not your thoughts, neither are your ways my ways, declares the Lord. For as the heavens are higher than the earth, so are my ways higher than your ways and my thoughts than your thoughts. "For as the rain and the snow come down from heaven and do not return there but water the earth, making it bring forth and sprout, giving seed to the sower and bread to the eater." Isaiah 55:8-10 ESV

But be sure to fear the Lord and serve him faithfully with all your heart; consider what great things he has done for you. 1 Samuel 12:24 NIV

Little children, let us not love in word or talk but in deed and in truth. 1 John 3:18 ESV

As he passed by, he saw a man blind from birth. And his disciples asked him, 'Rabbi, who sinned, this man or his parents, that he was born blind?' Jesus answered, 'It was not that this man sinned, or his parents, but that the works of God might be displayed in him. John 9:1-3 ESV

So to keep me from becoming conceited because of the surpassing greatness of the revelations, a thorn was given me in the flesh, a messenger of Satan to harass me, to keep me from becoming conceited. Three times I pleaded with the Lord about this, that it should leave me. But he said to me, "My grace is sufficient for you, for my power is made perfect in weakness." Therefore I will boast all the more gladly of my weaknesses, so that the power of Christ may rest upon me. For the sake of Christ, then, I am content with weaknesses, insults, hardships, persecutions, and calamities. For when I am weak, then I am strong. 2 Corinthians 12:7-10 ESV

But God chose what is foolish in the world to shame the wise; God chose what is weak in the world to shame the strong. 1 Corinthians 1:27 ESV

For the body does not consist of one member but of many. If the foot should say, "Because I am not a hand, I do not belong to the body," that would not make it any less a part of the body. And if the ear should say, "Because I am not an eye, I do not belong to the body," that would not make it any less a part of the body. If the whole body were an eye, where would be the sense of hearing? If the whole body were an ear, where would be the sense of smell? But as it is, God arranged the members in the body, each one of them, as he chose. If all were a single member, where would the body be? As it is, there are many parts, yet one body. The eye cannot say to the hand, "I have no need of you," nor again the head to the feet, "I have no need of you." On the contrary, the parts of the body that seem to be weaker are indispensable, and on those parts of the body that we think less honorable we bestow the greater honor, and our unpresentable parts are treated with greater modesty, which our more presentable parts do not require. But God has so composed the body, giving greater honor to the part that lacked it, that there may be no division in the body, but that the members may have the same care for one another. 1 Corinthians 12:14-25 ESV

For as in one body we have many members, and the members do not all have the same function, so we, though many, are one body in Christ, and individually members one of another. Having gifts that differ according to the grace given to us, let us use them: if prophecy, in proportion to our faith; if service, in our serving; the one who teaches, in his teaching; the one who exhorts, in his exhortation; the one who contributes, in generosity; the one who leads, with zeal; the one who does acts of mercy, with cheerfulness. Romans 12:4-8 ESV

From him the whole body, joined and held together by every supporting ligament, grows and builds itself up in love, as each part does its work. Ephesians 4:16 NIV

... and provide for those who grieve in Zion—to bestow on them a crown of beauty instead of ashes, the oil of joy instead of mourning, and a garment of praise instead of a spirit of despair. They will be called oaks of righteousness, a planting of the Lord for the display of his splendor. Isaiah 61:3 NIV

Each one should use whatever gift he has received to serve others, faithfully administering God's grace in its various forms. 1 Peter 4:10 NIV

Medical

Cerebral Palsy (Health Alert) by Ruth Bjorklund

American Heart Association (PDA)

What is Cerebral Palsy (CP) in Preemies by Cheryl Bird

Cerebral Palsy Guide (www.cerebralpalsyguide.com)

Other

She Reads Truth, Lenten Study by Rebecca Faires

Mere Christianity by C.S. Lewis

Disability and the Sovereign Goodness of God by John Piper

Celebrate awareness and victories of all abilities, ethnicities and ages through exceptional programs, outreach, and inclusion education. Break the Barriers, Inc. mission statement (www.breakthebarriers.org).

45210602R00055

Made in the USA
San Bernardino, CA
27 July 2019